YUKON QUEST

PHOTO JOURNEY

Photography by Laurent Dick

Text by Brian O'Donoghue

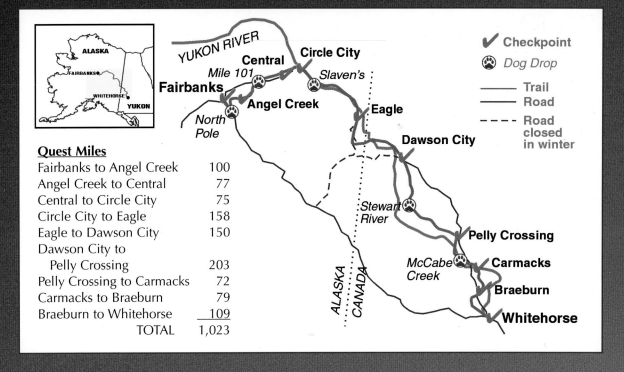

Quest Miles

Fairbanks to Angel Creek	100
Angel Creek to Central	77
Central to Circle City	75
Circle City to Eagle	158
Eagle to Dawson City	150
Dawson City to	
Pelly Crossing	203
Pelly Crossing to Carmacks	72
Carmacks to Braeburn	79
Braeburn to Whitehorse	109
TOTAL	1,023

International Standard Book Number 1578332192
Library of Congress Control Number 2002114953

Published by **Todd Communications**
203 W. 15th Ave. Suite 102
Anchorage, Alaska 99501-5128 U.S.A.
e-mail: info@toddcom.com
For additional copies of the
Yukon Quest Photo Journey, please send to the publisher:
US$ 22.95 (includes $3 postage and handling) inside U.S.
US$ 25.95 (includes $6 postage and handling) outside U.S.

Editor: Flip Todd
Designers: Sheila Bullington and Diane O'Neill
Text: Brian O'Donoghue

Photography: Laurent Dick

Printed by Samhwa Printing Co., Ltd., Seoul, Korea

10 9 8 7 6 5 4 3 2 1
First Edition

DEDICATION
To all who helped me in many different ways along and off the trail;
to all the race volunteers, for their tireless behind-the-scenes effort;
and to all those whose spirit is at home in the wild.

Laurent Dick

SUN DANCERS
*Japanese adventurer Keizo Funatsu crosses
Eagle Summit at dusk. The Yukon Quest
Trail winds through a vast wild expanse of
frozen rivers and treacherous summits.*

BEGINNINGS

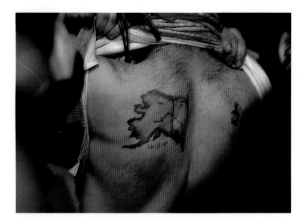

Some teams come from faraway places like Germany.
Others bring dogs bred in the surrounding Yukon forests.
All share dreams of their dogs' promise.
Triumphs possible, adventures certain.
A finish line 1,000-miles distant.
Most shudder;
they gird themselves for nature's fury.

⋀ REVEALING TATTOO – *Both the Quest Trail and his team's finishing time adorn Salcha, Alaska musher Mike King's back.*

⋁ COUNTDOWN – *Nenana musher Shannon Brockman, left, and race veterinarian Alan Hallman banter in the starting chute, down on the Chena River in Fairbanks.*

⋏ VARIED BLOODLINES—*Alaska huskies share thick coats, tough feet and the instinctive desire to pull. While purebred teams exist, most competitive kennels trace their lineage to generations of breeding experiments by traditional Native mushers and their modern counterparts.*

"DOG RACING IS KIND OF LIKE PLAYING CHESS. WHEN YOU PLAY CHESS WITH SOMEONE WHO'S REALLY GOOD, THEY MOVE A PIECE. BUT THEY ARE NOT JUST MOVING THAT PIECE; THEY ARE MANIPULATING THE WHOLE BOARD TO WHERE THEY WANT TO BE FOUR OR FIVE MOVES FROM NOW. AND THAT'S WHAT YOU HAVE TO BE DOING ALL THE TIME WHEN RACING." —*Bruce Lee*

⋏ GENTLE ANCHOR—*Volunteers provide a steadying influence in the Quest staging area while waiting to move a team into the starting chute.*

⋏ FLYING DEPARTURE – *Paws churn as Whitehorse musher Frank Turner, winner of the 1995 Quest, and the only musher to start every race in the Quest's first two decades, sets off.*

➤ FRONT ROW – *Mid-February temperatures call for parkas at the Quest's starting line.*

"I'm always worried I'm not making it out of the starting chute. It's pretty nerve-wracking — crowds, logistics. 'Do I have time to get my dogs bootied up?' 'Did I forget something I may need 500 miles down the trail?'" — *Peter Butteri*

"IF YOU START ON THE WRONG RHYTHM, IT'S GOING TO AFFECT YOUR WHOLE RACE. IT'S ALSO A BIT OF A MYSTERY WHAT THE RHYTHM OF THE COMPETITION WILL BE. YOU JUST HOPE THE RHYTHM YOU TRAINED FOR IS THE RIGHT ONE." — *Peter Butteri*

≺ PACKED FOR TRAVEL – *Dawson City musher Peter Ledwidge rides the runners of his fully loaded sled, gliding out of the starting chute.*

Ɣ RIVER GATEWAY – *Local cab driver Dave Dalton drives his Dalton Gang from Fairbanks, where crowds line the Chena River downtown. Teams generally leave the Quest starting chute in two-minute intervals, in a sequence determined by lottery. The race starts in Fairbanks, Alaska, USA and ends in Whitehorse, Yukon, Canada in even-numbered years. In odd years the race starts in Whitehorse and takes a slightly different route before ending in Fairbanks. This enables more villages to participate, while residents of Fairbanks and Whitehorse get a glimpse of the racers at both ends of their journey.*

RUNNING HARD

▲ PATCHED – *Salcha musher Jack Berry runs behind a broken sled, which sports willow poles lashed into place to offset damage to the rear vertical stanchions. Ingenuity in the face of adversity and self-reliance on the trail are Quest hallmarks.*

Freed from training rigors,
nagging concerns of modern life,
mushers and dogs set their own pace
on trails blazed by Jack London's kind.
Those hearty stampeders, fur traders,
pioneer mail carriers,
and other Yukon legends gone.

Days bleed into night.
Stars infiltrate trees.
Shadows play tricks.

But nothing distracts
from team and trail.
Run. Rest. Eat. Sleep.

Find the dogs' rhythm.
Then hang on for the ride.

▲ HIGH COUNTRY – *Nineteen-year-old Nenana musher Brenda Mackey chases a sunset across the top ridge of Eagle Summit. Both Mackey's father, Rick, and her grandfather, Dick, are past winners of Alaska's Iditarod Trail Sled Dog Race.*

◄ TRAFFIC STOPPER – *Volunteers lend a hand at a rare Quest road crossing.*

V HOLD ON – *Two Rivers musher Aliy Zirkle, the first woman to win the Quest, exhibits what mushers call the "thousand mile stare."*

WELL DRESSED – *Louise, left, and Tatchun share lead dog duties in German musher Petra Noelle's team near North Pole, Alaska. As conditions warrant, mushers will wrap light-weight coats on dogs susceptible to frostbite, or place fabric booties on dogs with sensitive paws.*

Λ FLUID ATHLETICISM – *Miles fall behind in a wave of rippling backs and a blur of charging fur.*

"I HATE WINDY TRAILS THAT ARE NARROW...YOU HAVE THIS SNAKE-LIKE GANGLINE AND THE FRONT OF IT USUALLY GETS AROUND OKAY BUT THE BACK OF IT ALWAYS GETS CUT OFF SHORT. SO YOU ALWAYS HAVE THE CHANCE OF RUNNING THE SLED INTO A TREE, OR INTO A BLOCK OF ICE." *— Walter Palkovich*

⋏ YUKON WORK OUT – *Keizo Funatsu, a Japanese musher now residing in Two Rivers, Alaska, wrestles his sled through brush as he negotiates an icy turn near McCabe Creek.*

⋎ WARNING SIGN – *Greenish or yellowed ice signifies overflow, a common hazard formed when underground pressure sends water spewing from cracks in the surface of otherwise frozen lakes and trails. Passing through fresh overflow can leave a team caked in ice. Worse, it sometimes conceals weakened river or lake ice, possibly even gaping holes, ready to swallow an unsuspecting traveler. Frozen overflow offers a slick, uneven surface, prone to sending dogs and sleds careening sideways.*

➤ ENCOURAGEMENT – *A snow-crafted map of the Yukon Territory boosts local favorites.*

Λ CHILL GLOW – *Ed Hopkins of Tagish, Yukon Territory rolls along the Pelly River on a clear 40-below morning.*

A FIRE BREATHERS – *The setting sun bathes a Quest team near Two Rivers, Alaska.*

"ALL OF A SUDDEN THE NORTHERN LIGHTS JUST LIGHT UP. THERE WERE THESE BIG PURPLE SHEETS RIGHT ABOVE US. ALL THE DOGS TURNED PURPLE AND THE SHADOWS WERE ALL OUTLINED IN PURPLE. I'VE NEVER HEARD THE NORTHERN LIGHTS MAKE NOISE BUT IT JUST SEEMED LIKE THEY SHOULD BE MAKING NOISE."

— *John Schandelmeier*

➤ NIGHT STALKERS – *Light reflected in the eyes of dogs betrays the approach of a team traveling in darkness. In benign sections of trail, mushers will often switch off their headlamps, saving batteries and savoring the moonlight. They rely on their lead dogs to follow rival teams.*

Ⅴ CELESTIAL SYMPHONY – *Northern lights flare in the heavens outside the Mile 101 Steese Highway camp.*

TEAMMATES

His pride, her fancy, stirs this endeavor.
Sleds decorated with sponsor's names,
one after the other,
angling for position in the pack.

Ambitions ebb on the hard trail.
Strategies splinter. Humbling,
enlightening supposed masters
to limits all creatures face.

Hardship brings recognition:
Pull together or fail.
Quest sleds are powered by trust.

⋏⋏ CRYSTAL WHISKERS – *Alder, a member of Frank Turner's team, wears the frosty effects of a sub-zero run.*

⋏ ALL TOGETHER NOW – *Two Rivers musher Jerry Louden labors forward, gripping his snowhook, poised to arrest the sled's descent if the team slackens its advance toward the crest of Eagle Summit.*

➤ KENNEL MATE – *Frank Turner has a few fond words with Buck, one of his lead dogs, during a rest stop at the Circle checkpoint.*

CHEERLEADER – *Marcelle Fressineau of Quebec plunges into her team during a playful pause in the action.*

SURVEYING THE COMPETITION – *Three-year old Red, left, and Swoop, an older wheel dog in Andrew Lesh's team, are intrigued by the other teams sharing a break at McCabe Creek, a Yukon Territory farm.*

▲ TROUBLE ON ICE – *Early in the 2002 race, Hans Gatt of Atlin, British Columbia faces a tense moment as his dogs break through the fresh overflow spilling across Eagle Creek. Gatt went on to win the race.*

◄ TAKING CHARGE – *Fairbanks musher Dave Dalton plays lead dog, guiding his team across a patch of glare ice.*

ꜛ PAW PATROL – *Sled dogs come to expect the frequent inspections essential for detection and treatment of foot problems.*

"MOST OF THE DOG CARE THAT TAKES PLACE ON THE TRAIL IS INVISIBLE TO ALMOST EVERYONE — IT TAKES PLACE BETWEEN CHECKPOINTS, WHERE THERE IS NO STRAW. YOU ARE JUST MOVING UP AND DOWN THE LINE OF DOGS ON YOUR HANDS AND KNEES, TAKING CARE OF DOGS."

— *Dave Olesen*

ꜛ TRAIL MEDICINE – *Louis Nelson Sr., an Inupiaq musher from the Kotzebue area, applies ointment to a dog's foot during a pause at the Eagle checkpoint.*

➤ SWEET TALKER – *Sebastian Schnuelle, a Whitehorse musher, nuzzles with a teammate at the Central checkpoint.*

PIT STOPS

Smell it?
Chimney smoke.
The invitation is enough
for a traveler with so far to go.

Bed the team in the cabin's lee.
First, the chores.
Check their feet, fire up the cooker,
mix another meal.
Only then does the driver relent,
yank open that cabin door.

Warmth floods. Smells fill the soul.
Stew fills the belly.
Refuge, gladly accepted.

⅄ GOOD AS GOLD – *Healy musher Dave Sawatzky fetches warm water for dog food from a propane-fired 55-gallon drum. The water is melted snow.*

⅄ MASS CAMP – *Lines of Quest dogs rest on straw at Mile 101 Steese Highway, a popular rest stop as teams next face an arduous climb over Eagle Summit.*

Ʌ CHOWING DOWN – *A dog in French musher Nicholas Vanier's team gulps down his meal of high-energy, fatty food. Most dogs in the Quest consume three to four watery meals and numerous snacks daily, providing the 11,500-plus calories necessary **each day** to fuel their performance.*

Ʌ MOVE OVER – *German musher Sylvie Furtwaengler cuddles with her dogs at the Braeburn Lodge checkpoint.*

➤ TRAVELING KIT – *Gear to be packed and supply bags acquired during this stop at the Pelly Crossing checkpoint await musher Amy Wright's attention. Prior to the race mushers pack food, dog booties, clothing and spare equipment in "drop bags" for shipment to eight checkpoints along the trail between Whitehorse and Fairbanks.*

∀ SMALL PLEASURES – *Brenda Mackey of Nenana dons clean socks at the Angel Creek Lodge checkpoint.*

◄ FORTYMILE HOSPITALITY – *Sebastian Jones, a volunteer from Dawson City, melts snow for dog water outside Fortymile cabin, a traditional Quest stop featuring coffee, home-cooked food and a hardwood floor cherished by tired mushers.*

◊ PLEASANT COMPANY – *Sig Stormo of Soldotna, Alaska banters with Native children at the checkpoint at Pelly Crossing, a Selkirk First Nation community, located roughly halfway between Whitehorse and Dawson, Yukon Territory.*

"IT WAS SO BAD AND THE CONDITIONS SO EXTREME, NOT ONE OF SEVEN MUSHERS UP ON AMERICAN SUMMIT COULD SEE ANY SIGNS OF A LIQUOR STORE."
— *Bill Steyer*

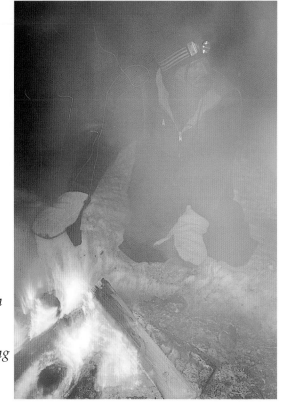

➤ CAUSE FOR PAUSE –
A clear, cold night finds Paxon musher John Schandelmeier, a two-time winner of the race, enjoying the bonfire at Stepping Stone, a farm outside Pelly Crossing, Yukon Territory.

Λ NATURAL REFRIGERATION – *Snowdrifts engulf a liquor store, Taylor Highway's lone commercial establishment on the ridge topping American Summit.*

Ʌ KEEPING TRACK – *Race volunteer and ham radio operator Kevin Abnett of Fairbanks sends race standings from Mile 101 Steese Highway using a computer-satellite link.*

Ʌ WARM WELCOME – *It's hard to miss Crabb's Corner café in Central, Alaska, a checkpoint where every musher is dished up a free steak for the asking.*

◄ GROUP EFFORT – *When Quest teams pass through town, roughly a third of Eagle's 110 year-round residents volunteer their services as checkers, cooks and custodians, staffing the town's old one-room schoolhouse.*

Ⅴ IN FROM THE COLD – *William Kleedehn, left, a German-born musher who makes his home in Carcross, Yukon Territory, enjoys a brew with former race official Dave Rich, right.*

Ⱥ WAITING GAME – *Volunteers at the Central checkpoint stand by to deliver supplies whenever teams appear. Vigils of this sort continue 24 hours a day as teams move largely unseen between the Quest's distant checkpoints.*

Ⱥ STREAKS OF PREPARATION – *Headlamps trace the movements of mushers preparing to pull out of Mile 101, with the northern lights dancing overhead.*

▲ NIGHT CHORES – *Fairbanks musher Andrew Lesh exits the old Eagle schoolhouse toting a bucket of water for his dogs and a can of alcohol for his stove.*

YUKON MILES

▲ ANCIENT ROUTE – *The Yukon River has long served as the region's main travel corridor, supporting boat traffic by summer and dog teams by winter.*

▼ QUIET SURGE – *Denali Park musher Bruce Lee cruises past huge Yukon drifts, launching the move that culminated in his 1998 victory.*

Canyon walls frame
the trailbreakers' beckoning groove.
Leaders prance, reveling
in the flat expanse.

Different spirits propel
the musher behind his sled.
He counters the Yukon's sloping pull,
eyes jutting ice, marks passing cracks.

He looks for telltale steam.
He reads messages writ in ice.
Below rush explosive torrents,
seeking frigid escape.

Madness, thinking about it;
impossible not to.

"Jumbled ice — you are going across there and your sled is banging back and forth. The dogs seem to be okay as long as you keep them slow, but the sled takes a beating and your body takes a beating, and usually the next morning your whole body is sore."

— *Dave Dalton*

◄ *NATURAL PROTECTION – German-born Sepp Herman, a Fairbanks musher, learned the value of a good fur ruff during years spent trapping in Alaska's Brooks Range.*

▼ *THREADING THE ICEFIELD – Bruce Lee gingerly drives his dogs through jumbled ice on the Yukon River. In 1998 and other years of scant snow, fields of icy boulders, stacked as high as 20 feet above the river's surface, form at virtually every bend in the Upper Yukon.*

➤ OPEN HIGHWAY – *The Yukon,
one of the world's largest rivers, has
its headwaters in Canada and winds
nearly 2,000 miles before reaching
the Bering Sea.*

⋎ GLASS BRIDGES – *Dawson
musher Cor Guimond crosses wind-
scoured ice near Eagle, Alaska.*

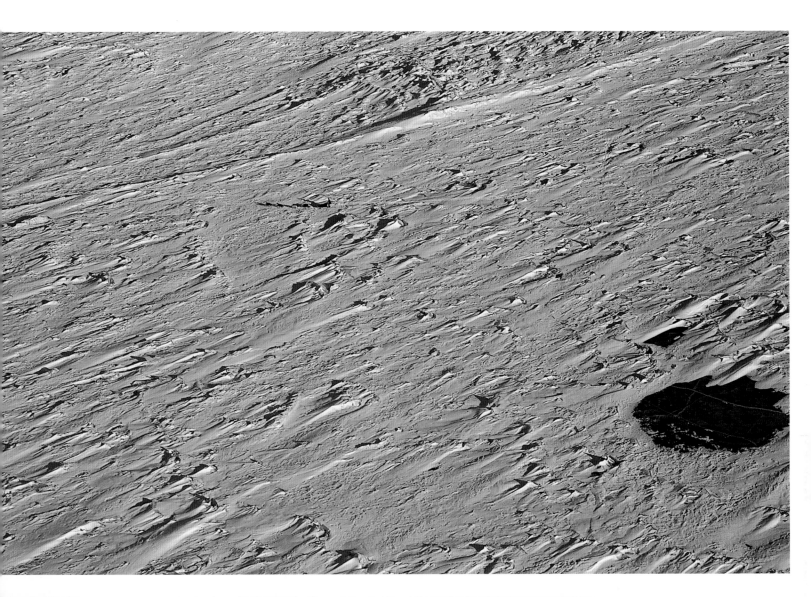

⋀ SMALL STEPS – *A Quest team, flea-sized in comparison to the icescape, proceeds down the Yukon's broad, rough skin.*

≺ CLIFF RUNNER – *Two Rivers musher Tony Blanford passes under a bluff from which nearby Eagle, Alaska took its name.*

ICY FRAME – Dogs driven by Joran Freeman of Two Rivers trot through ice shelves created by movements in the Yukon's seasonal skin.

⋀ SLICK RIDE- – *Cim Smyth of Big Lake, Alaska leans hard, striving for control during a passage through glare ice.*

➤ TRAVELER'S FRIEND – *Sunrise greets Wasilla musher Doug Grilliot's team near Eagle.*

"I THOUGHT I WOULD HAVE TWO WEEKS ON THE TRAIL TO THINK ABOUT AND RESOLVE SOME OF THE BIG QUESTIONS IN LIFE. BUT WHEN YOU ARE OUT THERE, THERE IS A CONSTANT BARRAGE OF CHALLENGES — ALL YOU THINK ABOUT IS WHO SHOULD BE IN LEAD. YOU WORRY ABOUT GLARE ICE OR HOLES PUT IN THE TRAIL BY MOOSE. YOU REALLY HAVE TO BE IN THE MOMENT."

— *Aliy Zirkle*

"IN THIS WILD AND CRAZY LANDSCAPE, NATURE PUTS A LOT OF CHALLENGES IN FRONT OF YOU. IT CAN FEEL LIKE A COLD AND DESOLATE PLACE, BUT WHEN THE SUN ILLUMINATES EVERYTHING, I'M REALLY HAPPY. YOU JUST CAN'T PUT A MONETARY VALUE ON IT OR EXPRESS IN WORDS WHAT IT MEANS TO RUN 1,000 MILES WITH YOUR DOGS. FOR ME, EXPERIENCES ARE MUCH MORE VALUABLE THAN BUYING THINGS." — *Shannon Brockman*

DAWSON RESURRECTION

Heaps of tailings,
rusting machinery,
skeletons loom
in the night.
Boomtowns lost
in rotting timbers,
a legacy of ruins
more eerie with each mile.

First to Dawson
claims gold nuggets;
a gesture appeasing ghosts.
The real draw: 36 hours of rest,
grub and help from handlers.

Famed Iditarod has its moments,
but nothing on the trail to Nome
bests Dawson's gift
to Quest-tired survivors.

ʌʌYUKON CHEER – *Dawson school children, suitably bundled for the occasion, provide a warm welcome for frosty dogs pulling Mark May, a Fairbanks musher by heritage, and veterinarian by profession.*

ʌ BOOMTOWN ROOTS – *The Klondike River town known as Dawson City grew like a weed when word spread that George Washington Carmack and two Indian companions, Skookum Jim and Tagish Charlie, discovered gold on Bonanza Creek on Aug. 17, 1896. Within two years, an estimated 30,000 to 40,000 stampeders were seeking their fortune at the camp located near the confluence of the Klondike and Yukon rivers. By 1910, Alaska gold strikes reversed the growth in the "Paris of the North," which at its height boasted opera houses, fine dining, saloons and dance halls serving miners with money to burn.*

∧ GOLD CAMP RELIC – *Down to six dogs pulling his sled, the minimum allowed, Fairbanks musher Dave Dalton approaches historic Gold Dredge No. 4.*

∨ STAMPEDE GRAFITTI – *Tailings spit out during the creeping advance of giant, gravel-eating gold dredges mark the valley floors near Dawson.*

"WHAT YOU STILL SEE OUT THERE REALLY JUST BRINGS THE HISTORY TO LIFE AND PART OF THAT IS THINKING ABOUT HOW PEOPLE GOT HERE IN THOSE OLD DAYS — CERTAINLY NOT WITH ANY OF THE HIGH TECH, WONDERFUL EQUIPMENT I'VE GOT, BUT WITH RAG TAG DOG TEAMS FED ON WHATEVER WAS AVAILABLE."

— *Brian O'Donoghue*

⋏ TRAIL DOCTOR – *A Quest dog receives a field exam from Marie Lim of Vancouver, British Columbia, one of many veterinarians volunteering their expertise at checkpoints.*

⋏ RECHARGING –
*Two Rivers musher
Bruce Milne delivers
food to dogs resting
inside a shelter at a quiet
campground across the
river from Dawson. The
shelter was erected by
handlers in advance
of his team's 36-hour
layover.*

⋏ WELL-EARNED REST – *A dusting of snow causes no stir among Quest dogs sprawled on straw.*

⋀ FINE TUNING – *Whitehorse musher Ned Cathers makes use of the Dawson break to slip fresh plastic on his runners, a measure aimed at reducing drag, making the sled easier for dogs to pull.*

⋁ SHEDDING WEIGHT – *Two Rivers musher Aliy Zirkle uses her axe to scrape the ice from the sled runners in Dawson, where gear is scrutinized for damage before teams tackle the second half of the race.*

◄ HANDLER'S LOT- – Walter Newman, a Fairbanks handler, cleans up straw following the departure of musher Keizo Funatsu. Assistance from Quest handlers is strictly limited everywhere but Dawson. For the most part, handlers trail their teams by truck, lending moral support at checkpoints, and collecting dogs injured or too tired to continue.

⋀ SETTING THE COURSE – The Quest and other long-distance sled dog races depend on snowmachine-equipped trailbreakers to break and mark the trail a few hours ahead of front-running teams.

MOUNTAINS AWAIT

⋀ PUNISHING ARENA – *When the Quest trail leaves the rivers, another climb soon follows.*

⋀ INTO THE STORM – *Lashed by winds reaching 60 mph, Two Rivers musher Aliy Zirkle urges her dogs through the six-mile passage atop American Summit's exposed ridge.*

Rosebud, Eagle, American,
King Solomon's Dome –
each of these mountains left its mark
on past Quests.
They separated champions
from the pack.
They compelled the weak
to quit.

Lead dogs display their mettle
or crumble.
Mushers find unexpected resilience,
or they, too, stall.

Summits care not.
Each, moody as the wind,
may pack a staggering punch.

⋀ DIGGING DEEP – *Whitehorse musher Doug Harris, a member the Royal Canadian Mounted Police, exhibits strain and determination on Eagle Summit's last steep pitch.*

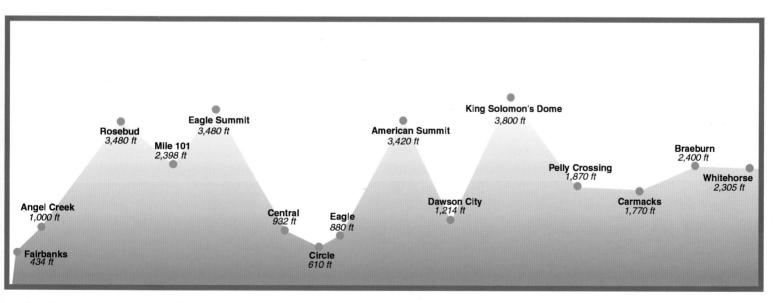

Eagle Summit
3,480 ft

Rosebud
3,480 ft

Mile 101
2,398 ft

King Solomon's Dome
3,800 ft

American Summit
3,420 ft

Braeburn
2,400 ft

Pelly Crossing
1,870 ft

Whitehorse
2,305 ft

Angel Creek
1,000 ft

Central
932 ft

Eagle
880 ft

Dawson City
1,214 ft

Carmacks
1,770 ft

Fairbanks
434 ft

Circle
610 ft

⋀ ROLLER COASTER RIDE – *Quest teams power up and down 1,000 miles of rugged mountain terrain.*

WHATEVER IT TAKES – *Aliy Zirkle of Two Rivers breaks trail ahead
of her team on the approach to American Summit.*

"I THINK THAT NOWADAYS YOU DON'T REALIZE HOW FAR A THOUSAND MILES IS ANYMORE UNTIL YOU TRAVEL IT AND GET TO SEE EACH HILL AND CREEK ROLLING BY YOU, AND YOU REALIZE JUST HOW BIG THE COUNTRY IS."

— *Gwen Holdmann*

Λ LONGEST PUSH – *Mike King of Salcha does what he can to avoid a stall on the long march up Rosebud Summit in the heat of the day.*

Λ RIDGELINE GLIDE – *Tagish musher Ed Hopkins cruises on the crest of King Solomon's Dome.*

≺ MOUNTAIN TRAIN –
*Paxon musher John Schandelmeier,
a two-time Quest winner and
perennial contender, breaks trail for
the lead pack ascending Eagle
Summit. This grueling passage
often proves decisive in years that
the race ends in Fairbanks.*

⅄ GOING DOWN! – *North Pole musher Mark May rolls off Eagle Summit, commencing a pulse-racing plunge through the Birch
Creek drainage.*

Ʌ NOSE FOR THE TOP – *A leader with admirable pluck guides Tok, Alaska musher Peter Butteri's team toward Eagle Summit.*

"IT WAS HORRIBLE. IT WAS REALLY STEEP LIKE IT ALWAYS IS, THE WIND WAS BLOWING AND I HAD TO UNLOAD THE SLED AND HAUL STUFF UP ON FOOT AND GO BACK AND WALK UP THE DOGS. WHEN WE GOT UP THERE THE WIND HIT. I WAS SOAKING WET, I FROZE MY NOSE, AND MY FINGERS WERE GETTING TOUCHY. IT WAS A PLACE WHERE I TOLD MYSELF, 'I HAVE ABOUT FIVE MINUTES TO DO THINGS RIGHT OR IT'S GOING TO GET SERIOUS IN A HURRY.'" — *Bruce Lee*

"YOU NEED TO BE IN TUNE WITH EVERY PART OF THE TEAM, MENTALLY AND PHYSICALLY. YOU NEED TO BE ONE UNIT. THESE DOGS ARE YOUR CLOSEST COMPANIONS, SOME OF THEM YOU HAVE RAISED SINCE THEY WERE BORN." — *Aliy Zirkle*

A GLOW OF ACHIEVEMENT – *Kris Swanguarin of Healy, Alaska charges across Eagle Summit's windswept plateau at sunset.*

FATIGUE

Dogs rest, oblivious.
It's the musher that's consumed:
tending paws, rubbing shoulders,
packing and cooking
another meal.

Sooner than later it hits:
the mind fogs, senses run amok.
Perceptions as simple as up and down
overrun with doubt.
Trail markers pegged in snow,
impossibly far apart.

Weariness nips at the driver's spirits.
Tiny setbacks assume dire proportions.
Choices breed dilemmas.

Rest, the obvious remedy, is a distant angel.
Grim certainty rules: the team needs him now.

⋏ PAST CARING – *The usually vibrant Cor Guimond of Dawson City reaches the point where it's more trouble than it's worth to remove even a headlamp or to unzip his parka at Slavins' Cabin.*

⋏ CONFRONTING THE WALL – *Aliy Zirkle of Two Rivers grapples with the effects of too many miles without sleep.*

"IT'S FINALLY CAUGHT UP WITH ME... I'M JUST KIND OF DOZING OFF ON THE BACK OF THE SLED, JUST TRYING TO HANG ON. AT ONE POINT, I WAS TAKING A BREAK WHEN THE DOGS SNAPPED THE SNOW HOOK, AND ALL OF A SUDDEN I REALIZED MY SLED WAS PULLING AWAY. BUT I WASN'T TOO ASLEEP TO RUN AFTER IT AND GRAB IT BEFORE IT WENT TOO FAR."

— *Frank Turner*

∧∨ FAMILIAR ORDEAL – *Frank Turner of Whitehorse, who has more Quest starts under his belt than any other musher, again conquers Eagle Summit step by agonizing step.*

▲ DEEP SLEEP – *Rest stops, timed to preserve a dog's speed and stamina, are essential for teams striving to compete in the Quest, an event requiring 10 days or more of supreme exertion.*

⋀ BUSHED – *Ned Cathers, a Lake Laberge wilderness guide known to eat coffee beans on the run, concedes this round to sleep deprivation.*

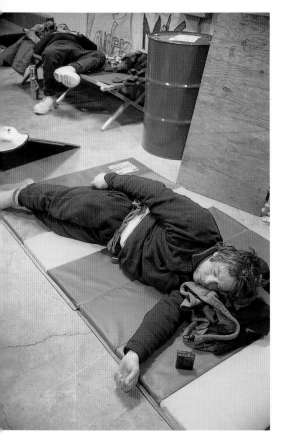

"THE HIGHER BRAIN FUNCTIONS WERE GONE. I COULDN'T REMEMBER ANY OF MY DOGS' NAMES. I THINK I HAVE GOTTEN THREE HOURS OF SLEEP SINCE THE RACE STARTED." — *Bruce Milne*

◄ ANY FLAT SURFACE WILL DO –
Jack Berry of Salcha naps without complaint on the floor of the firehouse in Circle.

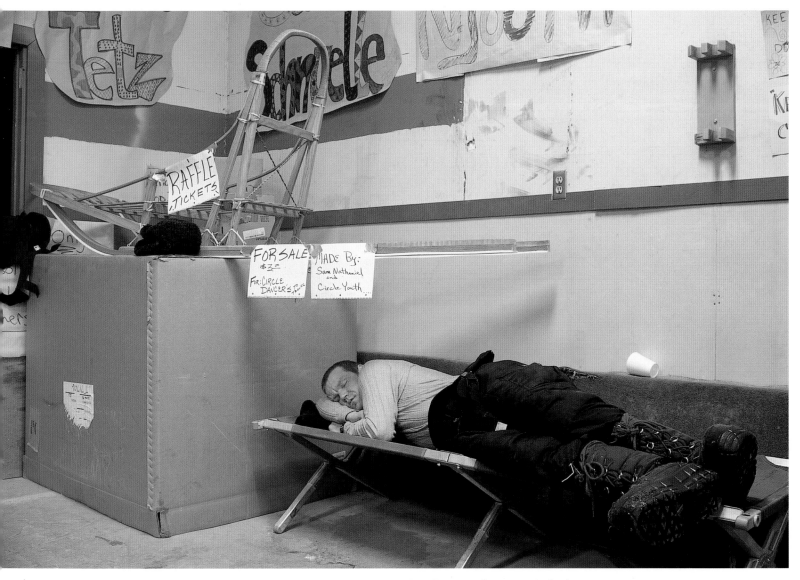

⋀ TOE WARMER – *Tagish musher Thomas Tetz didn't let boots slow his race for a Circle firehouse cot.*

FINAL PUSH

Crowned by dawn
or shadowed by nightfall;
met by one hunkering friend
or the camera lights' dazzle,
the sight of that finish banner
fills hearts to bursting, first to last.

The journey: 10 days for the swift,
18 for those less fortunate.

No matter. Canine or human,
Quest finishers bear changes.

They've more in common,
perhaps, with Klondike-era kin
than teams chasing dreams
out the starting chute.

⋀ SWIFT RISE – *Some doubted Keizo Funatsu of Two Rivers had the Quest trail savvy to sustain his team's impressive drive in the early miles of the race, but the man from Japan held on to capture top rookie honors in 1997.*

⋁ CHAMPION EDGE – *Hans Gatt of Atlin, British Columbia uses ski poles to supplement the dog power of his seven-dog string, a strategy that gradually ate up the competition in 2002.*

ʌ PULLING OUT THE STOPS – *Dave Dalton of Fairbanks sprints for Whitehorse on the Yukon River, running behind his sled in only double-layered wool socks. Dalton was 15 miles from the finish line when he shed his mukluks because the soft moose skin soles lacked traction.*

ʌ HOME FREE – *Healy musher Ramy Brooks was just 30 in 1999, the year he glided into Whitehorse first, becoming the Quest's youngest champion. He is the son of sprint-mushing queen Roxy Wright and grandson of Gareth Wright, another Alaska Native sled dog racing legend.*

➤ RESPECT – *Atlin musher Hans Gatt greets second-place finisher Peter Butteri, the musher he came from behind to beat in the final days of the 2002 Quest.*

⋏ LICENSE TO GLOAT – *Tim Osmar, a wily fisherman from Ninilchik, nets his first Quest crown in 2001, a race decided when Dave Sawatzky's dogs faltered on Eagle Summit.*

"WHEN YOU FINISH THE RACE WITH THE DOGS, WHEN YOU HAVE GONE THAT FAR AND YOU HAVE DEALT WITH ALL THE DIFFERENT THINGS THAT HAPPEN ALONG THE WAY, YOU ARE NEVER THE SAME. IT HAS A PROFOUND IMPACT, I THINK, ON MOST PEOPLE."

— *Frank Turner*

⋀ FINISHERS FROLIC – *A pair of purebred Siberian leaders arch their backs in the finish-line snow, savoring the completion of their journey with Wasilla musher Wayne Curtis.*

⋁ MUTUAL ADMIRATION – *Wayne Curtis and a four-legged comrade from Stormwatch Kennel share affection in Whitehorse.*

▲ I DID IT, DAD – *Doug Zirkle shares daughter Aliy's victorious moment in Whitehorse. While only one team takes the big prize, every musher completing the race brings home a sense of achievement and renewed appreciation for the dogs shouldering the load.*